Secrets to Happy Home Selling

Insider Secrets to Preparing and Selling Your Home for the Best Price and Terms without all the Stress.

By Cyndee Haydon

First Edition, 2017

www.SandbarsToSunsets.com

Published by Sandbars To Sunsets Inc. under ISBN:

ISBN 13: 9780999191200

DEDICATION

For you…when it's time to prepare, market and sell your home. My hope is that you find this book of value.

TABLE OF CONTENTS

ACKNOWLEDGMENTS

I want to thank my loving husband and partner in life and business, Jack Haydon for always supporting and encouraging me – you make it all possible.

I also want to thank Charlotte Volsch and Kim Ward for being my friends in our Mastermind Group because we get things (including this book) done…together.

A special thank you goes to Kit and Mark Whittington, featured on the cover, who started as ideal clients and have become dear friends and dream buddies.

INTRODUCTION

DON'T WORRY – BE HAPPY

Life Changes...and with it so do our homes. While growing up, my family moved almost every two years eventually landing in Tampa Bay. These experiences helped shape who I am, how I choose to live and how important it is in my business to keep things as simple as possible for our clients while achieving their goals.

I wrote this book to help you, today's home seller, so that you can make the emotional shift needed and help you prepare while transitioning from a homeowner mindset to a home seller mindset. You can feel comfortable because you will know what to expect, how to prepare yourself, prepare your home and ultimately take out much of the stress of this process.

In this book, I focused on the three things that home sellers frequently tell me they want:

- to sell their home for the highest price,
- in a timeframe that works best for them,
- and to do it with the least amount of stress

My purpose is for you to be outrageously happy with the help my team and I provide you while we help you understand the necessary steps and are the guide by your side through the entire process of selling your home.

You will find home selling preparation tips and successful strategies to avoid costly challenges and mistakes. You will benefit from the lessons and yes insider secrets I've learned from being a real estate advisor since 2005 and helping hundreds of buyers and sellers. Most importantly I'll share real stories (though the names have been changed to protect their privacy) and real experiences of other home sellers like you, so you may begin the transition of thinking more like a home seller yourself. This includes understanding the journey and the magnitude of what you're about to undertake.

Putting a sign in the front yard or deciding to sell and putting your home in the MLS is the easy part. Choosing the right real estate advisor to personally commit to getting you and your family calmly prepared for and through the process is the unpredictable hard part.

It's often the intangibles that you'll come to value most. Things like communication, patience, responsiveness, accountability, resourcefulness, problem solving, listening and strong people skills that can be hard to quantify. Hearing what others have to say about their experience however, is a good place to start.

So, as you read this book, you may come to better understand the value of hiring an experienced real estate advisor like me with a knowledgeable team. In today's real estate market, it's not just getting an acceptable offer that means success because experience shows, one in five homes that go under contract and never sells; you can't count your chickens before they hatch or your proceeds before closing day! Don't be that one in five.

It's all the hundreds of complexities most people don't know or they assume won't happen to them. It's been shown that it's always in the last 100 feet that you will either be jumping for joy and celebrating success or experience the heartbreaking emotional rollercoaster and financial cost of failure.

One thing is for sure, home selling is an emotional, complex process and money is an emotional topic. Occasionally, I hear sellers focusing on how little they want to pay someone or how they can even do it themselves. This can cause a lot of unnecessary stress. It's better to focus on how to make the most money, with terms and timeline that work for you by choosing a proven guide by their side, like me, to guide and get to the celebration of a sold home.

I'm not going to tell you that you get what you pay for because you already know that. Today there are some "low cost looking" models available to home sellers and it's often confusing because who wants to pay more than they have to... right?

Real estate advisors, like me and my team, work on a contingent fee. This means we invest all our time, our money and our expertise in getting your home sold. We do all the work, incur all the expenses and only get paid when you are successful. We never just "take listings" because we actually get homes sold and we'll discuss why it's important to understand the difference more inside this book.

As you flip the pages and read, I hope you'll be able to see behind the curtain of the Wizard, and take away some of the mystery of home selling. This book gives you a better, deeper understanding of what it takes to sell your home for the most money, with the best terms and the least stress in today's challenging real estate market. You'll discover there are two paths:

- you can decide to take the risky one with little support
- or you can choose the "easy button" working with an

expert

When your values are clear,
your decisions become easy.

May your home selling journey
be an easy, low stress and
successful one!

CHAPTER ONE

How to Sell Your Home for the Most Money:

When Opportunity Meets Preparation

The purpose of this book is to give you a better understanding of the journey of selling your home for the best price with the least stress possible. This chapter will expand on this and give real-life examples, and proven strategies on how to best accomplish this goal. Learning how to prepare a house to sell for top dollar quickly is no easy task, so I applaud you for taking the time to learn more about the process.

The following strategies and insights can be used to help you make better choices with next steps in this process. Let me just say, if you love chaos and drama this book is definitely not for you. However, if you are someone who wants to know how to avoid any added turmoil then continue reading!

Start by asking yourself "What is important about selling this house to me?" You may find it helpful to write you're your answers and keep it posted somewhere that you will see it often. I like to post important reminders on my bathroom mirror or refrigerator. If you have a clear understanding of why you are selling, it will help give you focus throughout the preparation, the marketing and successful sale of the house.

Once you have decided on your reason(s) for selling you can then start working on your timeframe and the Smart Home Selling Process.

Our Smart Home Selling Process:

- Hire a Realtor®
- Room-by-Room Review
- Pre-Listing Inspection
- Cleaning & Repair
- De-Clutter & Depersonalize
- Staging and Photo Preparation
- Soft Staging
- Take Professional Photos
- Pin-Point Pricing
- Coming Soon Marketing
- Full Launch Marketing
- It's Show Time!

The Smart Home Selling Process is a step-by-step guide to getting your home from where it is now, to being prepared, to begin the marketing phase. You, as the seller, will play a large role in deciding on the timeframe for this process.

Once the home has been de-cluttered and cleaned, your real estate advisor can then begin the marketing stage. The marketing stage includes soft staging, professional photography, and all the advertising that the property is for sale.

Experience shows that the work done in these early steps can result in a 10% or greater increase in what buyers are willing to pay, which is why we address these topics first when we discuss getting the highest price possible. All the negotiation skills in the world won't change a buyer's emotional attachment or desire to want your property. In fact, it is usually the intangibles that move buyers to make their best offer. Many buyers will be educated on the feature, function, benefits and value of the house, but it really comes down to how they feel about the property.

The Preparation Process

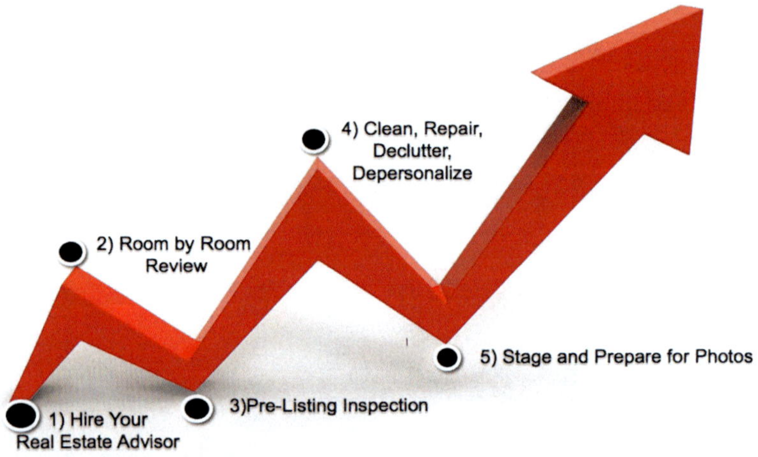

When we begin to focus on what we need to do to get the highest price, with the most value, leading to the biggest return on your investment, we start by thinking about what differentiates your home from the competition. This is an important step, because no one sells their home in a vacuum.

With all the information available through the click of a mouse, your home can be compared, at any given time, in many different ways with whatever else is available in the current housing market. Anyone can access this information including appraisers, who are part of the buyer's loan process for the purchase of the property. This is why the objective should be to make your house stand out to as many buyers as possible. It is why the Preparation Stage of the Home Selling process is so important.

What we find most often when working with someone selling their home is that it is important to first step back, take off your rose-colored glasses, and take an objective look at your home as it is right now. Then decide what needs to be changed to make it look like what we want it to look like once it is on the market. By that I mean, decide what do you think you need to do to:

- depersonalize and de-clutter?
- identify repairs needed to quickly and easily prepare it for sale?

Once you choose me and my team to help you, we will go into more detail on each of these steps to guide you through the process.

During the Home Selling Preparation Process your real estate team goes to work doing all the things that make your home a box office hit. We want it to be the high return investment that you're looking for then follow with The Home Marketing Process.

The Marketing Process

The Home Selling Journey is made up of the Preparation process to defend your equity and the Marketing process should be comprehensive so your home attracts buyers willing to pay the highest price and offer the best terms.

The Home Selling Journey

Now that you've glimpsed at the big picture to start your home selling journey you can see why most people start thinking about, and begin preparing to sell months before they want to move. Keep in mind that the first, and most important step, is to hire a real estate advisor you trust to guide you through both the Home Preparation Process outlined above.

Completing the Home Preparation Process means that everything you need to do to get ready to move into the marketing phase of home selling is complete. This is why it is so important to have a skilled professional real estate guide by your side from the very beginning.

Real estate advisors, like me, who do this every day can also be invaluable in letting you know what repairs and improvements to make and, just as important, what won't provide a good return when selling. Most home sellers are surprised to know that many of the most impactful things cost little to no money. Let's take a closer look at the various steps in the marketing process.

The 70- 30 Rule

Most people living in a house have 70% of their items decorating and filling space in the home. That leaves 30% actually showcasing the desirable features of the house. Look around your home right now…what do you think your ratio is? It is totally natural to surround yourself with all the things you love. But when selling a home, the ratio should be only 30% your belongings and 70% actually showcasing the home's features. This way you are highlighting the strengths of the house that will attract the next buyer.

This is our focus in the Home Selling Preparation phase – you are transforming space in your home that is filled with what you love, what identifies you, what identifies your family, what makes this "home" to you, and bringing the focus back to what we're marketing - the house.

To defend your equity and get you the highest offers from potential buyers we need to reduce your personal belongings. By reducing your personal family items to 30%, space is then opened up to welcome real homebuyers in the market to see their belongings and their family in that new space.

This proven process consistently helps our clients make their home more appealing to more potential buyers. Doing these steps up front can not only make you more money, it also reduces stress by selling the home faster and proactively removing issues rather than waiting until after a willing buyer has viewed the home.

The Room-By-Room Review

To start the process of reducing your personal items to 30% take notice of the things that are unique and specific to you, such as your interests, your hobbies, and your collections. I've worked with many people who have vibrant personalities, and they will reflect that vibrant personality in their home. When placing a house on the market it is best to go with subtle and neutral features over vibrant ones. Choosing neutrals will attract the most buyers because it allows each person to see themselves and their belonging working in the space. That is the goal, to allow each buyer to fall in love with a house by seeing themselves living there.

To simplify the process, we have developed a plan known as the Room-by-Room Review to help homeowners. This plan prevents overwhelm and analysis paralysis by dividing the home into sections allowing you, the seller, to minimize your stress.

In the next section of the book we have included a series of before and after photos of our Room-By-Room results, which lets you see the impact that small, orchestrated changes can make.

There are three parts to the Room-By-Room Review:

- viewing through the eye of the camera
- pre-listing inspection peace of mind
- the emotional magic of soft staging

We make time to go through your home with you, inside and out. We look at each room and what is currently in it. Then we look at how to make the rooms stand out from the competition. You decide as we go through – are you going to:

1. Throw away?
2. Give away?
3. or Pack it away?

Doing this for each room opens up the space, allowing us to stage, and to create the desired effect we want in each room.

Through the Eye of the Camera

To reduce the overwhelm of preparing the home for sale, we go room-by-room together. In the first part of our Room-By-Room Review we're considering an eye on how we can create more of a blank canvas, and definitely a neutral canvas to be able to tell the story of your house. When we're finished you have a working plan enabling you to address one space at a time. You see the impact of what you're doing to enhance the features of your home. To get the plan in place we will discover the unintended distractions the camera will pick up and then consider what we want the buyers to focus on in each room.

I've found that it's really helpful in this process to actually use the camera on my phone. I even have a wide-angle lens to take a picture of each room similar to the professional photographer's lens. I do this so that we can capture the true picture of each room because it's been proven that our minds edit. We know that when we get the home ready for market, it will be online through photos and the camera will not edit it. I've discovered that even when I am coming into a home, often my mind will edit unintentionally. It's really important that we get a good sense of things that may be drawing in people's attention. We can then determine if what draws someone's attention is the focal point that we really want. It surprises a lot of people when we use the camera as a checkpoint. They can see what the room really looks like to someone else and not what they see when they look at the room.

This is a simple tip you could do right now. Go to a room you think looks great and take a photo. See if the room looks as great in the photo or if you find yourself looking at something on the floor or something on a nightstand versus seeing the whole room. This is why we always take photos as we're going through the room-by-room review. We are looking at it with an eye toward what we should move to another location or remove completely.

Pre-Listing Inspection Peace of Mind

Next, we are looking for what needs to be fixed, repaired, or enhanced. All of these things are really an important part of our ability to defend your equity and ultimately get you the best price. Why? Because every little repair, every little flaw in a buyer's mind triggers their natural inclination to exaggerate the repair costs. Some research has found that buyers assume the cost to fix something is typically ten times more than it actually turns out to be and they want compensation for it. It's always better to fix what you can up front. Every little detail we can take care of before opening the front door for homebuyers is going to make for a much smoother process throughout the transaction.

This is why we do a Pre-Listing Home Inspection. Even the most conscientious homeowner can have things that need to be fixed in their home. It's so much better to find out now and take care of cost-effective repairs or be able to disclose defective item in writing rather than to have them derail your sale. We may not discover everything because we won't be crawling into the attic or under the house, but we will look at the interior and exterior of the home together. Experience shows that it really helps increase buyer interest.

We will next determine what items you want to fix and what you want fixed by a handyman. Another benefit is that taking care of these things up front can be done more cost the task is too much for you, you will have the help you need versus the hard task of doing the work alone. effectively because you are choosing the plumbing fixtures, lighting, flooring, etc. Once you're under a purchase agreement, the buyers may request all work be done be a licensed professional which I don't have to tell you will always cost more.

And finally, if there are items that you're not going to fix, you are able to disclose that on the seller's disclosure. It may sound simple, however we all have quirky things in our homes that "have always been that way" and we just forget. You don't want a home inspector to make a mountain out of a mole hill or have the buyer start getting an uneasy feeling about the condition of the home. Telling the buyers up front shows honesty and builds trust.

Example Repair List - 123 Main Street

Preliminary Staging

- Pack all personal photos
- Living room-move white table from entry into corner of living room
- Remove rug
- Remove all stuffed animals and minimize pet toys
- Kitchen-remove magnets from refrigerator and minimize items on the counters
- TV room-move sofa under window, pack and store personal property
- Office-pack unused items and tidy up desk areas
- Patio- remove cover from table and chair set

REPAIRS/TO-DO

Exterior of home

- Hose down or power wash exterior including fascia board and eaves
- Wash and spray paint security screen door
- Replace white motion light at exterior of garage
- Replace damaged ceiling fan in garage with a white light
- Paint front and north side fencing (dark brown)
- Install dark brown mulch in planter beds
- Continue to water front yard
- Install outlet cover at west side of garage
- Paint cover at rear patio by electrical panel (white)
- Replace vertical blinds at sliding door in living room

Example Repair List – 123 Main Street (cont.)

Interior of home

- Paint exterior of front door (blue)
- Caulk master bathroom shower
- Clean track of sliding glass door so that it slides easier

Items to Purchase

- White exterior light for garage
- White interior light to replace damaged ceiling fan (garage)
- Ceiling fan (master bedroom)
- Two globe lights (master bathroom)
- Mulch for planter beds
- Exterior cover for electrical outlet
- Vertical blinds for living room sliding door

Schedule handyman that we recommended to help with repairs

Schedule professional cleaning company that we recommended

Clean – Repair – De-Clutter – Depersonalize

Now that we have completed the Pre-Listing Inspection and the Room-By-Room Review you have a specifically crafted plan on what to do to prepare your house for the market. We can also help you with a list of trusted vendors who specialize in everything from deep cleaning to home repairs. We can even provide you with a referral to individuals who specialize in de-cluttering and depersonalizing the house. That way if

This is a time when I like to remind my sellers that when we do everything right you can expect to sell your home in 30 days or less. It's worth the preparation, so why not get packing now when everything is less hectic than it will be once you're under contract for the sale.

I won't to go into much detail because each home gets a very specific preparation plan. I will share that if you only choose one thing to get your home ready it should be white glove clean. Most buyers believe clean equals well maintained, and not clean equals not maintained. If your home is not clean, experience shows that buyers will immediately start looking for the homes weaknesses. My experienced recommendation is doing whatever it takes to clean up thoroughly. This includes the most overlooked items when preparing a house for sale and that is the windows, so take the time to detail them. Remember, because we work with professional photographers they will be shooting through the windows to bring the outdoors in and those windows must sparkle! Even if you have to hire a window washer, my best advice for you is put your best foot forward by having a very clean home.

As far as repairs, we will work with you to determine what must be done based on your specific situation, what makes financial sense to take care of, and what to disclose and let the next owner determine how to handle.

The Emotional Magic of Soft Staging

The third, and final part of the Room-By-Room review is creating an emotional attraction to the house. This is what all potential buyers are looking for; to feel the excitement of this is home. To help visually attract homebuyers, my team has been trained to use a technique called soft staging. The best way to explain soft staging is taking what is available in the home (or what we have stored in our staging warehouse) and creating vignettes that sell the lifestyle potential buyers are wishing to lead. Buying is an emotional process. What my team and I do as our seller's trusted real estate advisors, is bring that emotional and magnetic attraction to each room, so buyers "feel at home".

Your home can subliminally become more attractive to buyers with just a few strategically placed items. This is why we suggest you team with a real estate advisor that is a marketing expert rather than your average real estate agent. When you hire a marketing expert, like me, before we ever place your house on the market we are at work using proven strategies to market it to sell quickly and just as important to sell for top dollar.

A picture is worth a thousand words and I've created a few examples so you can see how the Room-By-Room Review can make your house more visually attractive to potential buyers.

Solids for School Pictures and Bedrooms

Do you remember when you were a kid and your parents prepared you for picture day at school? Or when you ever had a family photograph? What's the first thing a photographer tells you when preparing for these events? To wear solid colors! Why? Because solids will "stand out" in the photo better then prints and patterns. As the subject of a photograph we look best when we wear solid color, and the same is true for each room in your house.

A lot of times homeowners will have bedspreads with patterns and prints and it's distracting and sometimes can distract buyers. A dynamic change can happen in a room when you take a neutral colored bedspread that is complimentary with the room paint color. It can be a very inexpensive purchase that will highlight the room and make it stand out. It is just like when you see your childhood school picture and you're wearing that solid shirt, you show well, and that is the same for well-staged room.

When selling your home, it becomes a house and it is no longer about what you like. You are presenting the house as a product and in the master bedroom the goal is to make it feel like a relaxing retreat. Need a visual? Just imagine a 5-star hotel room and if you're not sure, Google any of the major hotel chains. Hilton, Holiday Inn, etc. and you can check out their room photos online. Those nice hotel rooms have solid colored bedspreads that look clean and crisp. In our own homes our bedspreads can be comfy and we love them because they're comfortable but worn. But this can cause your buyer to subliminally equate worn with dirty. Buyers are looking to buy a "new home" with a "fresh start"; presenting your home as crisp and clean is always a winner. We are creating the effect of walking into a hotel room; that "ahhhh, I can relax here, this is my sanctuary, this is tranquil, and inviting." It's a simple tip that has a huge impact when the camera is marrying the look of the room to the emotion created in the potential buyer.

Some of the basics to consider for bedspreads are white (but not when you have white walls), beige, navy, grey and a punch of color like blue or green in kid's or guest rooms. The master bedroom bed should have four pillows stacked two and two. For added excellence add an accent pillow or two. The key here is the bedspreads usually don't have to be expensive – I've picked up full queen or king sets with shams, pillows, and a dust ruffle for $75 at Ross, TJ Maxx or Target. Trust me, it's $75 well spent and the really nice thing once you successfully sell your house, you get to take it to your new home.

Master Bedroom Before

Master Bedroom After

Take Me Away Calgon...

Bathrooms even when they're dated are one of the most important rooms in the house.

First and foremost, they must be clean, clean, clean! Nothing will get a buyer running from your home faster than a bathroom that feels yucky!

In older Florida homes, it's not uncommon for us to go into bathrooms that may have sinks or built-in items from the 50s 60s or 70s that might have teal green, pink or other colors. The way we minimize that is go to the hotel formula, which is white equals cleanliness, fresh and relaxing.

In the bathroom featured here you can see we had a lot going on in the before picture from a patterned shower curtain, variety of artwork, variety of personal hygiene items on the countertop, bath rugs and more.

Here's an example of the magic of our soft staging and room-by-room analysis and preparation is around creating positive emotions once you've done what must be done, ...it must be clean no matter what!!! Then we went with the basics and added a white cloth shower curtain, some luxurious white towels, and yes you knew I had to add something green, something living, something inviting...

Did you already notice the delicate orchid on the back of the toilet? I bet you did. It adds a pop of color pictures and it also serves another purpose, which is to draw buyers into the room.

As we said before when it comes to selling a home you need an expert marketer that happens to have a real estate license to be the guide by your side because we know the tips and tricks and

Bathroom Before

Bathroom After

secrets to making your home look its best, to making an appeal to the most buyers and evoking an inviting positive emotion that makes buyers "attracted to" your home.

This home happened to be a home where the owner had recently passed away. We helped their family prepare and get it ready to go on the market. As you can imagine, this is a hard and emotional time under any circumstance and when a loved one passes it's even more important to have experienced, caring advocates working for you.

We were able to help them know how to get rid of things; helped stage and prepare the home for the professional photographer and the market.

The soft staging you see is not expensive – it's just knowing what to buy and how to pull it together to get the desired effect which is where my certification in staging comes in handy.

The result was that this family ended up getting multiple offers and top dollar for this home in a way that was as comfortable and stress-free as possible under the circumstances.

In the last few years as the market has rebounded experience shows that a home that has been properly prepared, staged, and photographed professionally is typically selling at 10% more than others that skip these steps - What could you do with an extra 10% when you sell your home?

Before adding Green

After adding Green

Green - the Color for Money and Life

Another important tip you cannot underestimate is the power of having something green or simulated living in several rooms of the house. If you don't have a green thumb, you can simply use artificial plants. When artificial plants don't fit you, it could be as simple as a green vase or some other item that's green. Since we've de-cluttered and created that blank canvas, now we have to make sure that the environment doesn't feel sterile. A simple green silk plant or some fresh flowers add a lot on photography day.

Now that I've share this tip with you, the next time you're in a staged home, at department stores or other decorated places you'll likely notice that there's always something green.

Some other elements from nature are seashells or twine balls that people may notice and subliminally connect as living items.

Knowing how to use these subtle vignettes and strategically positioning inexpensive accessories are not the kind of things the average real estate agent may have studied and mastered. From knowing how to show a vibrant room in photos to creating the space that feels alive when buyers walk into it is what my team and I can do for you.

Office Before

Office After

It's Showtime – Lights, Lights, and More Lights

The final soft staging tip is to check all your light bulbs. Make sure that you have the highest wattage light bulbs in all your lighting. All lights should be plugged in and working. Buyers are naturally attracted to brightness; if you've watched any home tv shows you always hear the compliment of "the home is light and airy." Create the feeling of sunlight because people tend to feel happier when there is light. If you have any rooms that are dark because of the angle of the sun or because of trees, really let the wattage of the light bulbs work for your house. We are basically bringing the outdoors in and creating that really bright feeling.

Occasionally sellers will say to me, "This is so bright and it's brighter than I'm used to," yes, it is and think of it just like when you go to the theater. On the stage those lights are bright because we want to see the actors; we're creating that same effect. When we do everything right, those homes are in demand and sell quickly. Remember this is your house's show time and we are creating the atmosphere to let your house shine!

You will be outrageously happy with the preparation because we are differentiating your house so that your investment, your house, will crush the competition.

One of the things that surprises my clients is they often think they're simply hiring someone with a real estate license. Over time they come to appreciate that what makes the difference in their experience is that choosing an advisor who is a really strong marketer and negotiator begins with preparation. That's why we

Living Room Before

Living Room After

spend whatever time it takes to prepare the house before we take the next steps.

A Picture's Worth a Thousand Words

I shared that I often use my cell phone camera to capture the before photos during a room-by-room review. These photos are just for the beginning and I would never market your biggest investment using those photos. We have professional photographers and we work together to capture what I like to call the money shots.

I am always looking for the money shots in each house and I make sure our photographer gets them.

As we're going through the house, I already know who are the most likely buyers. And as we go through, we've talked about the different examples: will it be somebody that is probably going to have a growing family, or is it someone that is looking to retire here, or is it an investment? We then make sure we're highlighting those features visually to them.

Outdoor Living Before

Outdoor Living After

Telling Your Home's Story

Now we are ready to skillfully craft the story. Each house has a story that we're sharing with the next owner. Our job is to couple your story with our knowledge of the market and consider what buyers want, what they are looking for, and how to best convey that to them.

We've talked about how it all starts with the staging, then the photography, and it moves into the marketing arena. We apply our market knowledge, and then do the pinpoint pricing. We look at:

- how does this house compare?
- what are this house's strengths?
- how do we minimize any weaknesses?
- how to best compete?

We differentiate between the potential buyer objections, which we can handle, and the property condition, which we cannot change, but can minimize. As a last resort, you must be prepared to mitigate with price.

For example, if you have a house that has a small yard, there's nothing that can be done to change that. But, because of our marketing knowledge, we know how to highlight the stress-free living a smaller yard offers. We focus on the positives of a lifestyle doing things you love rather than having to spend all your free time doing yard work. We market each house appropriately to attract the person who is going to appreciate that feature versus someone who won't.

Oceanfront Balcony Before

Oceanfront Balcony After

Lifestyle and Views =Money Shots

Compare the two photos and notice the simple touches in the After picture that make this small space more inviting, more memorable, and helps buyers imagine themselves in this space.

We put some brightly colored pillows on the patio chairs. This pop of color conveys that happy feeling and a focal point when taking professional photos.

We also made to sure to add something green and this time we had a small potted plant in a green pot in the center of the table so it feels alive, welcoming, and inviting and on the lounger we put a pillow along with a luxurious towel all of which to say... "I've saved you a space, come relax, welcome home!"

When you have a view whether they are on the ocean, on the bay, on a lake...it is a huge selling feature to buyers. An experienced real estate advisor like us, will help you highlight and focus on this feature. This is what I call the money shot!

When you are selling a property whether it's a house, a townhouse, a condominium or a villa.... you are really selling a dream! Buyers are dreaming about the memories they will make, the good times they will have and the enjoyment they will gain by living here.

It's important from a marketing perspective to understand when is the best time for prospective buyers to see your property. If your property gets sunset views you'd like to make sure potential buyers experience that.

Master Bathroom Before

Master Bathroom After

Making Your Home a Box Office Hit

We've already learned that what's most important for home sellers is that they have an expert marketer and negotiator that just happens to have a real estate license! When you have this combination, you have someone who is looking at everything through a unique lens. Let's put the emphasis on how my team and I can professionally present this home as a box office hit. We focus on our plan for the grand opening with the red carpet rolled out that is going to be so attractive that many buyers are going to be lined up to see it first. That's what can happen because you're choosing a team who knows what potential buyers want and know what's going to capture them.

We are building the scene, writing the script, setting the stage, making sure everyone looks their best with primping and make-up and then the director captures it all on film. When it's all done the teasers come out to let people know it's coming soon, to build up the excitement and then the big day is here. The red carpet is rolled out and since we've done everything right, you experience big financial results, fast. When it comes to your house the goal is multiple offers in the first week; especially when we're in a strong seller's market.

Hitting the Bulls-Eye with Pinpoint Pricing

We can start working early on with you to prepare; however, we won't know a pinpoint price until we know when you're ready to put it on the market. We know some people will take a year in the preparation phase, some people will take 6 months, some people will take 3 weeks, and some people will take a week. Each timeframe will require a different timetable to get it all done and we are going to discuss "time that works best for you" in one of our next chapters in much more detail.

Feel comfortable knowing that we can work with you in the timeframe that works best for you which we will address later in this book.

As you get closer to being ready and your home being available for buyers to purchase, just know the market is ever changing.

It's dynamic like the ocean. It ebbs and flows. To get specific we need to know WHEN you want to go to market.

When you're ready, then we take all that information and we can build a plan to say here's right where your home is and here's right where the market is going to receive it well.

So now you're ready to put your blockbuster home "on the market" – now it's time to determine the price of admission. We start by reviewing all the information that impacts what the highest price is at any given time. You'll compile a detailed list of improvements you've made especially those in the last five years for us because those will bring the most value on an appraisal.

We look closely at the current competition, we look at what's currently under contract and what's sold in the last 180 and 365 days and we build our case for buyers and appraisers, too, so they see the value! We discuss and decide how to adjust for any items that you decided not to fix. We talk about what conditions exist that can't be changed and will ultimately impact the price; for example, the home being on a busy road, a bad view or in an airport flight path.

We take all this information and with all our experience help sellers zero in on a real pinpoint price of where the market is when they are actually ready to hit the market.

People pay more for things they perceive are a good value, desirable and special – it's that "It Factor" and we all know IT when we see IT. We've been making the buyers feel that way about your home through the whole preparation process (where we decided to throw it away, give it away or pack it away to get to our 30% while making needed repairs) as well as differentiation from the competition (using emotional vignettes and using soft staging, positioning, photos, marketing, pinpoint pricing and more).

You can hopefully understand now why the Preparation stage is so important as well as the Marketing stage – these give the biggest return for the least expense!

One thing sellers don't realize is every time we help a buyer and many of the times when we help sellers we can get a copy of the appraisal to review.

Why do we do this? Because we can see the exact amount appraisers are consistently adjusting for various items like extra bedrooms, a one car vs 2 car garage, a swimming pool or not, a view, a fireplace, bathrooms and more.

It's really difficult for a real estate agent to defend your equity if they don't know these values and how to work them for your good. This information helps us give you, the seller, advice on how to focus on the right things. The focus in order is:

1. things that are necessary
2. maybe some of the things that would be nice
3. things to just leave alone because the value isn't going to be recognized

It's so important as a home seller that you are investing in the right things and not spending money at this stage that you won't get back.

All of this chapter is about getting your home on the market; however, it's our strong negotiating skills that ensure that the buyers and the appraiser see the value and you end up at closing with every dollar you deserve. To end up with the most money possible, you really need to find an expert marketer and negotiator with a real estate license who has the time and attention to dedicate to your success. I am that person!

CHAPTER TWO

Timeframe that Works Best for You: Reasons for Selling

Timing

When you decide to sell your home the first thing you must consider is what is your timeframe… the timing that works best for you. Timing will drive everything else. From there we can help you build a strategic, specific action plan to make it happen.

Timing means different things to different people. I see the range from, "I want to sell immediately, how quickly can we get it on the market and sold?" to "I'm sort of in the three to six months timeframe," to "I am looking at my next chapter and that could be one or two years."

Regardless of whether it's something that you've been thinking about for the last thirty days or have thought about, talked about, mulled over for the last year, you'll appreciate sitting down for an hour with an experienced guide by your side to help prepare you for your journey.

What I've noticed is when it's an immediate life experience that makes it necessary to move quickly, it's a relief to know that someone is going to help take care of all the details. These are the details that you may not know about or simply don't have time for because you still have your full life.

For example, if someone passes away and you're responsible for their estate, you still have your life and your family to take care of. It could be that the property is in another city or state and there are details upon details that must be taken care of. Often there is a need for an immediate relief to have this all handled. Knowing you have the help you need with my team because we present your options and you make all the decisions is priceless. To get it all done while you're going on with your life and keeping you informed of the process, allows you to feel comfortable and meet the time frames that are required by the estate.

When timing requires you to move quickly, having experienced professionals, your attorney and your real estate advisor, handling details while you travel elsewhere, can be a relief. When I am your real estate advisor, you can be where you physically need to be while critical details are being handled. This includes all the frequent and necessary communication to you every step of the way. My process presented an enormous relief for seller Jacqueline through her relocation from Florida to Ohio. Her house was on the market a mere five days after she left for Ohio, and it was under contract four days later.

It's important to have someone come in and look outside of your scenario to consider a few different options to think about in that planning stage. That way when you're ready to say, "okay, go! we're ready now", we've been thoughtfully planning, you really are ready. Really ready means all of the things in preparation have been done to meet your timeline and price needs, which creates a smoother transition. Most importantly, this allows you to move only once.

Knowing why you're moving is a big piece of the timing equation. When you have children, school start times are important. In the case of a divorce, we often experience as a more immediate need. Relocation can be impacted by the new employment date; you get the point. Every scenario has its factors and working within the factors is our plan.

Upsizing

When we think about selling, where we're going next frequently has a big impact as to the time frame that we choose.

An example that I would share is when my clients are transitioning from one planned stage of life to another. Creating a larger family by having more children comes to mind and as a family is growing they may be outgrowing the home. The thought is often we need a bigger home or maybe we want to get the children into a different school district.

Downsizing

Another example of a long-range plan is when you are considering downsizing from your current home to something smaller or single story. Clients usually know a year or two in advance because they are planning to become empty-nesters or retiring and they start to think about moving to a home that fits the change in lifestyle and the next phase of their life. Sellers have shared with me that they most often are thinking about that one, two, or as many as five years ahead. They begin to examine what is on their horizon, where they are considering moving to, and their next steps.

Relocating

Relocation is usually because of a career move and typically within a 6-month time frame. Things start happening within the company and the relocation department usually is letting you know details. The good news is that you've got some time to know where you're going so that you can make some plans. Sometimes people don't reach out until they're really six months or so away from the move. I've discovered there are two kinds of individuals in this scenario and my husband and I tend to be both sides of it. Using the example of shopping for a car I am the type of person who really doesn't want to look at the models or know what I should do to prepare until I am in a position where I can take real action. My husband, on the other hand, likes to research, touch, compare and see what he can do to prepare for the inevitable purchase.

I've experienced a segment of people who when it comes to selling their house begin the plan six months in advance. They start to say, "okay now we're ready to talk about tangible plans and get concrete advice of what we should be doing." In my experience, approximately 75% of people fall into the category of planning months ahead for their move.

Divorcing

When couples find themselves in a scenario where they're going through a divorce, and need to sell the home to split the proceeds allowing both parties to move forward to their next chapter, the timing is often referred to as "quickly". It could be as quickly as wanting the home on the market in 30 days or less. Being able to give practical concrete steps to have the house ready, in the time frame that works for them, and to be able to give numerous resources to help them achieve their goals is something that's been invaluable to couples that find themselves in this situation.

Only Moving Once

I believe this to be one of the most complex situations that we experience. When clients are deciding whether to buy first or sell first, it is timing, and the ability to accommodate those moving parts requires a lot of skill. It's crucial to have an experienced, detail-oriented team to ensure that all the "i's" are dotted and the "t's" are crossed and that communication is high and systems are in place for precise timing.

Having an experienced real estate professional, a guide by your side, will keep you out of the danger of crash landings that can have a major impact on your equity and your timeline.

Imagine all the many moving parts; especially in today's information and technology era. You can get into information overload and this is when you need accurate answers. Having someone, like me, to get you answers, quickly, and avoid turbulence is an important part. A safe landing is our goal. It's important that you know that coming into the last hundred feet (the successful closing of escrow), that's where it gets fast, furious and very precise. You can feel comfortable that I will be your pilot, and you can relax knowing that my team has all the details handled.

Financing

You would be appalled at the number of people who because of the lack of good advice, proper planning and steps, are unable to purchase that next home. What a nightmare when they've sold their home with the traditional real estate agent who doesn't work with the right financial people to make sure that all of the right pieces are in place. That's been a big surprise for people who have great credit scores and have never had a financial worry in their life.

You'd be surprised at how cumbersome this can become without proper planning. Knowing the right steps and how to realistically time everything making for a smooth transition, but happen in a less stressful way is really important.

So, you've not only timing factors, financial factors, landing factors, but many key points as part of the transaction. Everything is happening in that last hundred feet and needs to be handled correctly every step of the way.

Sell First Then Buy

My team and I recently helped a family wanting to sell their home and buy another one because the wife's parents were moving in with them. The newer home was beautiful and in a great location. The home needed minimal preparation and could be on the market in a few weeks.

It was important to John and Alice to plan around their two children in elementary and high school because they wanted the whole process to be as smooth and stress free as possible for the children. When we discussed their timing, we discovered they were most comfortable selling their home first and then buying their next home.

After we talked about how in this competitive real estate market in order to get a seller to accept their offer with the contingency of them selling their home, it usually means giving up something favorable in the terms or increasing their purchase price to offset the added risk to that seller. John and Alice wanted to be able to make an offer without the contingency of selling their current home.

They were also worried that because they were selling their home in a strong seller's market with fewer than usual number of home sales, meaning fewer comparable properties and with their home being one of the nicest in the area, they may have an issue with their home appraising for the purchase price.

Once they were on the market, they relied on my guidance and experience to evaluate various buyers' offers and to understand the impact of each of the terms, as well as what they would net from each offer. They decided that for their peace of mind and planning they would go with the cash offer that didn't require an appraisal because I had educated them on the strong possibility that there might be appraisal issues due to lack of good comparable homes in the last 6 months near them. It also means that once the inspection period was over they could start making the financial commitments they would have to make to move to an apartment without worrying if something might go wrong with a buyer's mortgage later in the process. It made for a smooth process that was comfortable for their entire family. They later shared with me how thankful they were that they were able to avoid the emotional rollercoaster that a co-worker had experienced during the selling of their home.

John and Alice understood that most appraisers will only give a value or adjustment of about $10,000-$15,000 for a pool even though theirs was gorgeous and had cost them over $40,000 just three years earlier. Smart buyers know that if a home doesn't have a pool it's going to cost them $30,000 or more to put one in.

This is just one example of why an appraisal is not what a willing buyer would pay for a home. It's important to know that appraisals are an art, not a science, and the most significant variable is what similar properties have sold for within the past six months. Appraisers prefer properties within 1/2 mile of the subject property, within up to 20% of the size and then they make adjustments from there. An appraiser rarely knows if the price of a comparable home was lower because the person living there had to sell because of a life changing issue like divorce, death or relocation.

As an advocate for our sellers, we make sure to educate appraisers on the "backstory" of comparable homes, as well as all recent improvements, so that our sellers' homes get the highest possible valuation. Appraisers are busy people and because we know the neighborhood better than they do, it's worth the effort to compile this data for them. It assures a much better result for our seller. A side note is that I have not had a bad appraisal in almost 10 years.

Buyer Financing

What you may or may not know when you're on the selling side, is that while the buyer has submitted an earnest money deposit, they have a financing contingency in the contract. What that means to you is that the buyer can still have a glitch with financing and this contingency allows them to cancel the contract and get all their earnest money back.

At this point, as the seller, you are usually pretty far into the sales process. In the scenario of John and Alice, they had to be moved out of their house within the time allotted in the contract. They had to commit serious non-refundable money to obtain a short-term rental including first and last month's rent and security deposit (over $10,000 in their case). They also needed to begin the packing, selling of some personal property and preparing for the moving process. Most sellers are using a moving company, and they have to schedule and commit to that as well. They also began to have carrying costs of two properties - the one they own and the one they've rented. These financial implications are why it's so very important to have a guide by your side to help make decisions that minimize the risk and costly mistakes that sellers can experience.

Back to Preparation and how it Impacts Timing

When considering timing, what we can help you understand is realistically what can get accomplished in what time frame. Sometimes this means while you might be perfectly capable of doing things yourself, to help shorten the timeframe you may choose to outsource tasks to someone else and enable us to get to market quicker.

Many improvements go a long way to defending equity and it's important to have the home prepared. The proposed timeframe will determine how it gets done and we can help with prioritizing. We can also help when by introducing trusted vendors to you because sometimes it's less stressful to have someone else do some preparation.

Jason and Camille, wanted to sell their home in Madeira Beach. Their decorating style was already very updated, neutral and appealing to most buyers. To help the buyers imagine themselves living there, I helped Jason and Camille to depersonalize. There was a list of things that needed to be repaired and they asked for an introduction to a handyman. Once the repairs and a bit of painting were done I helped with minor, yet buyer emotionally impactful staging. I loaned them a new bedspread and made sure we had something green in every room. I recommended they move an entry table to a different location in the living room. We needed enough time to get professional photos, as well as time to prepare their customized marketing plan so that everything was ready when we came to the market with the maximum exposure. The good news is from the time they chose to sell, to having the home on the market, was just ten days.

We take care of our selling families throughout the transaction process. Selling a home can be one of the most stressful things one does in life.

So how do we minimize stress?

The timing is often like a pressure cooker so we get organized and make sure that things don't explode. We know how to get you through the process in a calm, organized way, and get help when you need it.

Having a skilled, experienced, and focused guide by your side who can lay out some different options around timing is critical. I will help you determine the time it would take for you to do it yourself, including material cost, and then weighing that out against the estimate of someone else doing the work. That way you can see how much of your valuable time versus paying someone else and whether you want to do that trade off, or not. You'll have concrete comparisons so you can make that best choice. It's all about what's most important to you while you are selling the property. It's our job to give you two or three good options that you can choose from and then you can then choose what would be best for your family and your specific situation.

It's Never to Early to Start This Process

The average home seller, according to statistics, sells a home every twelve years. Having someone, like me, that knows the selling process, can help you to understand what to expect, and being that resource plus advocate is important. I've discovered that having information early in the process makes it an overall better situation for sellers, because you want as good of an experience and a great outcome, don't you?

I recently received a phone call from Mary because she and Bob were updating their kitchen. They had no plans to sell, but they talked about how they might move to a different house in a few years. Mary said, "we are thinking about these very unique lights over our kitchen counter, what do you think?"

I told them that if they like the lighting, that they should install them and enjoy them. Because they may not appeal to most buyers when they sell the home in a few years, they might need to replace them. Changing the lighting would not be a huge expense but, if you want to balance the cost to update as trends change that is also something to consider. So I mentioned they might look at something that fits their personal taste, but that was less taste-specific. They appreciated just having somebody to ask so they could make an informed decision before they invested their hard-earned money.

You can only imagine how disappointing it would be to think that the improvements being made will increase the value of a home, only to find out that is not the case. The good news is that you can avoid that scenario by having me as your go-to person, your guide by your side.

CHAPTER THREE

Selling with the Least Amount of Stress:

Having a Guide by Your Side Helps to Reduce Stress

In this Chapter, we cover selling with the least amount of stress while dealing with highly complex situations. I've mentioned selling your home can be one of the most stressful events in life. Most of the stress is created because of dealing with unknowns. Having a good communicator as your guide is critical. It's important that you understand the market, the pricing, and the preparation. I keep you updated and informed every step through the selling process. That's important for reducing your stress. The selling process is very time sensitive, and with frequent updates you will be able to respond quickly. This ensures you don't miss any opportunities to defend your equity.

Having to Respond Quickly

Technology is one of the best ways to really span those depths and distances. Stress comes when you get an offer, especially in timely markets. Whether it's a buyers' or sellers' market, people are looking for quick responses before they move on to another property. The ability to get that information in front of you, the seller, whether you live locally or in another area by using technology is critical. Often couples are both employed and may not have the time to communicate about the preparation and sale of their home every day. By using technology, the smart advisor gets the same message out to both parties so they can reply with all their questions. This type of communication helps ensure that the timeline required to respond to the buyer isn't missed. Plus, everyone knows what is happening. Everyone is getting the accurate answers to the questions, so that everyone is well-informed of the next steps.

Not Knowing

Our human mind immediately goes to negative or guarded thoughts when we are in situations of not knowing. For example, if you come home today expecting your son or daughter to be there and they aren't, we usually don't think, "oh I'll bet they stopped to give a friend a ride home after school and they'll be here any minute." We usually are thinking some horrific thing has happened and an uneasy anxious feeling comes over us.

As we help people with selling their home, the biggest financial choice of their lives, we are very sensitive to the need for them to be communicated with regularly. The communication includes what is happening now and what is happening next, to eliminate the stress of "not knowing".

To make communicating complete, it is imperative that your advisor really listens to what is being said and how you are saying it. This way the reply and the response are appropriate to your need. You may need help right now, or someone to listen, or be searching for a solution and reassurance. All of those different things come into play at different times. Experience shows that when you have a guide by your side who is competently handling the unknowns and communicating what they are doing, you feel confident and this brings relief. My team and I have got you covered in this journey with the biggest financial choice of your life.

Simultaneous Closings

One of the most complicated situations occur when a seller wants to sell their current home and close on their new home quickly. Orchestrating a seamless process of closing and buying is an art form. There are many moving parts, each impacting the other, and the opportunity to have something go wrong is significant.

Nancy and Juan were getting a divorce and needed to sell their home. Selling a home can be one of the most emotionally stressful situations. Adding a divorce to the mix requires a really skilled negotiator, like me, to skillfully manage the negotiations of both transactions. Nancy had already moved out and taken a job in another city. Juan would be buying another home close by. Juan had three challenges. One, he needed the proceeds from this home to buy his next one; two, he had a dog; and three, their teenage daughter was also living with him.

Juan wanted the move to go as smoothly as possible, and just as important, for his daughter's sake, he wanted her to feel little disruption in her life. It was also very important for Juan and Nancy to work with a real estate advisor that they could confide in, yet trust to keep things confidential.

Juan and Nancy, never expecting to sell so soon, had completely remodeled their home in the last two years. When we launched their home's custom marketing plan and it hit the market, we received multiple offers. We negotiated and they chose the offer that worked best…for them. We simultaneously began helping Juan find his next home. Even in a strong seller's market, we were able to negotiate a purchase agreement contingent on the sale of their home.

Everything went smoothly until the appraisal came in low because there were no other homes to compare it to; homes that had sold in the last six months. Because we had helped them choose well-qualified buyers and had discussed this possibility with the buyer's agent up front, we had a Plan B. The buyer had already agreed to do a cash out refinance on their primary home and pay cash for this home. So, while this closing would be cash, it meant some additional time was needed for the refinancing process. The buyer's lender thought they might need an extra day to be ready to close.

While a day may not seem like much, needing an extra day when you're doing a simultaneous closing means coordinating lots and lots of details in a tight window of time. It can be challenging to make sure you don't lose the home you're buying by missing the contracted closing date. This is where working with a real estate advisor with a good reputation and good negotiating skills can make a huge difference. The other issue is movers are usually booked weeks out so it may mean packing as planned; however, as a seller, you may now have an extra day of holding or storage of items unless you can do a pre-occupancy with the home you're buying.

In this case, we negotiated with the seller of the home that Juan was buying to agree to the delay and the movers worked with Juan to come one day later. Juan was very happy that we were able to smoothly close the next day.

Home Repairs

The National Association of Realtors or NAR says the average person moves every twelve years. Getting a home ready including finishing needed repairs can be overwhelming because frequently people don't know who to trust and what repairs will give the best return. Then there is the scheduling and supervising the work to be done. We can help to reduce your stress of repairs because of our experienced and organized team. We have trusted plumbers, an electrician, handyman, several painters, a landscaper, a tree trimmer, etc. Helping the seller press the easy button is our goal.

Sellers have shared that the hardest part is not really the expense for the preparation of their home for sale. The hard part is knowing who to trust to do the work and getting on their schedule. We've found that because we have worked with the vendors previously and established a good working relationship, our clients often become the vendors' priority. When we tell the plumber, the handyman, the landscaper that we need the work completed in a timely fashion, they honor that.

Frank recently called me to tell me he had tried to call three electricians to get a quote and no one would even return his call. The electrician that we gave him not only returned the call but showed up when they said they would. The electrician asked Frank to send pictures ahead of time so they could be fully prepared. They showed up on time, did the work and Frank called me to say "Wow, what a difference in treatment, and thank you for the introduction."

Buyer Home Inspections

Many of us have lived in our homes a long time. Some sellers are surprised that some things aren't working. Much of the time they've forgotten it doesn't work because "it's always been that way".

When buyers make their offer, they are expecting a well-maintained home. The buyer's home inspection is when in a matter of hours, the buyer's love affair with your home goes from engagement to wedding plans, or they get worried.

That's when having an experienced real estate advisor, once again, becomes critical. Remaining calm and having conversations to discuss concerns is an art. Having the ability to negotiate a win-win to address what has been discovered is a skill. This is when you need someone, like me, to oversee the details because you want to avoid your home going back on the market and everyone wondering "what's wrong with this house?"

Title Issues

It's very important to have a title search completed before going on the market. Issues are frequently discovered and most sellers are completely unaware of existing title issues. Most of these title issues simply require time to have them corrected. We don't want to discover something that will take three weeks to correct once we have negotiated a purchase agreement. When we find a problem ahead of time, we have the opportunity to get it cleared up.

Preparing and Moving

I think it's critical that you know the value the whole team brings and how much you have to gain with our support in this process. You're not alone because being alone through this process can be a daunting task including deciding where to start. You can know that we will help you plan what to pack, and what to keep for staging. We're different because we don't take your listing and then leave you to figure out the next steps. We are team and as such, before we install the for-sale sign, we work together towards preparing you and your home.

Divorce

A common situation is when couples, uncouple. The scenario of preparing and selling a home when divorcing can be very challenging. There has to be some agreement on contracts, on terms, and then there has to be agreement on house preparation and who's going to be taking what. Because there is a certain amount of tension in a relationship that is ending, when combined with the stress of preparing the home, packing, and moving you get a lot more additional stress.

One way we make our sellers more comfortable and less stressed in the planning process is to help them craft their story of why they are selling their home. We do this because it's the first question that every Realtor®, every person that looks at a home, and even your neighbors are going to ask, "Why are you selling your home?" We help our client have a comfortable response without revealing any motivation that would impact the ability to sell the home for top dollar.

If a couple is getting divorced and it is not common knowledge then we might suggest answering that question of why are you selling with, "We are relocating," which they both definitely are. As we discussed earlier, you want a real estate advisor with excellent marketing skills, who can customize a plan to showcase your home's best features and benefits, while helping to get top dollar by not letting buyers think that there's an angle they can use to pay less.

Finding a Buyer

Because we work with so many buyers we know people that are looking in the neighborhood for properties. They are constantly in communication with us.

When selling, all you really want is a buyer. The biggest thing we can do to alleviate your stress is to lay out the plan for how we're going to find that buyer. You can relax because my team knows what to do to find you the right buyer because that's what we've been doing for many years.

Contract Terms

Not knowing what contract terms mean can be stressful generally just from a lack of understanding. You will appreciate that we take the time to explain the terms of the contract, including the impact of the buyer's requested timeline. Understanding the negotiation and finding that win-win allows us to make sure any items that don't work for you, the seller, are addressed in a counter-offer. We always keep in mind what is important to you, the seller, and ensure that you have enough time to pack up all your things and comfortably get to your next destination.

Having Committed to a Buyer Who Can't Close

A buyer who can't close poses incredibly large ramifications to the seller who hasn't considered this possibility ahead of time. Sellers often don't understand the problems until they're in a situation where there are no options. A common nightmare situation is a buyer who can't get the loan a week before closing the transaction because they didn't have a pre-approval with a solid lender. I always speak with the lender to make certain the lender has researched the buyer's credit, verified income and provided proof of funds needed for down payment and closing costs. I do this so that we all understand the depth of the pre-qualification. Once we have negotiated with a buyer, we have a timeline for inspection, appraisal and removal of all contingencies. What this means to you is that I am overseeing everything to be absolutely certain the buyer and their agent are working towards removing all contingencies. Experience shows 97% of the time, once all the buyer's contingencies are removed, the transaction closes escrow. I am able to oversee everything that is happening because my team has a system with checkpoints. These checkpoints are to the seller's advantage to be certain the transaction is progressing according to the purchase contract while protecting the seller so they don't experience costly consequences.

Recently we were referred to a couple who were in their 80's and looking to sell their home of 22 years and move closer to their adult children. They had placed a deposit on a home in South Carolina. Because it was a sellers' market we knew with our preparation and marketing their home we would be under contract quickly. The first weekend we had over 20 showings and received multiple offers. The first offer received was full price. Our clients were ready to sign; however, I encouraged them to wait until I could speak with the buyer's lender. I knew what they didn't … that one in five offers accepted doesn't close and often it's because of financing glitches. I always want my clients to feel comfortable, but I knew it would be better if my sellers had one restless night rather than to accept the offer. Especially because they had many other buyers interested in the home. I asked them to trust me. I wanted to make sure they were not stuck in a contract for thirty days only to possibly be more stressed and disappointed if the buyers were unable to qualify for a loan. I explained to them that it was better to wait now than to have everything packed and already to close on their other home, only to find out that this buyer for their home couldn't close. They agreed to wait, and when I called the lender the next morning I learned that that the buyers were self-employed. While they were doing great with their businesses, the hurdle was that if the lender used the normal two tax returns filed, their loan wouldn't be approved. I also learned this mortgage broker was changing companies in two weeks which is why the buyers had requested 45 days for the loan commitment. These are the type of hurdles that can be addressed early on, when the right questions are asked.

Because I do this every day I knew to ask more questions and get a better idea of the risk involved. When I saw them the next morning they looked terrible and told me they hadn't slept all night. They said the stress of all these showings and not having a buyer under contract for their home was much harder on them than they ever thought it would be. I shared what I had learned with them and that we had another offer, a better offer, and that while I hated to have them lose a night's sleep being so worried, I was thankful they weren't going to be disappointed later. They were very thankful that I was protecting their financial and emotional interests.

There's nothing that creates stress like big financial surprises. All this work, all this planning for the big day of celebration, and to have the rug pulled out from under you at the last minute, is just emotionally devastating to most people. Our goal is to make it look easy and feel stress free. That is mastery, many years of experience, and systems plus great teamwork that makes it feel easy, which is what we strive for.

It's really that last hundred feet that makes or breaks it all and that is where the biggest financial consequences come in. Being left with a vacant house and still making mortgage payments because something goes awry and moving quickly because of transition commitments can cause double the stress level because of all the financial issues. Many clients are needing the proceeds from one house to take them to the next place. They don't have thousands and thousands of dollars sitting there to fill a gap in case there's a whoops.

Those last hundred feet are when the big whoops can happen, sometimes causing one or two extra mortgage payments or an extra fee for the storage place. When a delay happens, you might have an extra fee for the moving, or because of scheduling you might end up without a moving company. There are a lot of moving parts in those last hundred feet. If you don't have the right person managing those moving parts, things get dropped and it's expensive.

It's similar to asking the professional plumber to come in and repair the problem because the sellers tried to do it themselves and created a flood. The plumber came in and used his special screwdriver and it was fixed and they say, "$150? you were here for only 15 minutes and you turned the screw that much." The plumber says, "I knew which screw to turn and how far to turn it and we see what happened when you didn't."

Realize that as a seller you have a lot of control before you accept an offer. Once you accept a buyer's offer you can be stuck with little or no options until the buyer doesn't perform. You have a lot more risk financially and a lot more potential for emotional stress.

Not Knowing When to Pack

Once they have accepted an offer, most sellers can expect around thirty days or so to be handing the house keys to the buyer. The buyer has approximately three weeks to complete their inspections, have an appraisal and obtain full loan approval. During this three-week period, the buyer essentially has a "free-look" at purchasing the home. As the guide by your side, I am monitoring each step of the transaction and making certain that the contracted timelines are adhered to.

I recently helped clients sell their family home and we were very diligent about the contract terms; however, the buyer was using an out of state bank for their loan. As you can imagine, this almost always adds to the complexity and stress of the transaction because each states rules and lender processes are different.

Experience shows the odds of closing drops dramatically because of communication issues with the lender employees. In this case although we made frequent phone calls, leaving voicemails and sending emails, we struggled with a delayed appraisal by more than a week, causing a delay in the buyer's full loan approval. This totally stressed the sellers knowing that if the house didn't appraise the buyers may not be able to buy it, and if they started packing early their home wouldn't look it's best if it had to go back on the market.

By the time the loan was fully approved, the sellers had only one week before they were to vacate the home. This is one of the reasons selling a home is naturally so stressful. Even when you do everything right, you are not 100% in control, and not everyone has the same ethics and honesty during the transaction. It's somewhat like playing chess, having to think 3 or 4 steps ahead and it's critical to have an experienced real estate team as your guide by your side help you throughout the transaction.

DID YOU KNOW?

State Law requires the Seller of a property to disclose to the Buyer all know facts that materially affect the value of the property being sold not readily observable or known to the Buyer.

What to Disclose

Helping people understand the seller disclosure forms can alleviate a lot of stress. Some sellers might consider putting minimal information down on the forms. It's important to take the time to go step-by-step answering all the questions and checking the boxes that apply. If you're uncertain, then simply ask your real estate advisor. I can help you to understand the purpose of each question on every document. By doing a thorough job, you not only fulfill a requirement, but you protect yourself from future issues.

No matter the condition of the home and its defects, the right thing to do is to accurately complete the documentation and provide the information to the buyer when they are excited about becoming a homeowner. It's the surprises after becoming a new homeowner that make the buyer have buyer's remorse. Helping you with disclosing everything you know about the home is another way that we relieve stress during the process because it keeps you feeling comfortable, and moving the transaction forward in a methodical, calm, planned manner.

Moving with Children

Another thought about the last hundred feet and dealing with less stress in highly complex situations is transitioning children into new schools and making sure that the timing is such that they get to the school when planned. It's very challenging for the kids and the parents to move to a new environment including school. Our purpose is to manage the transaction so that the children get there in enough time to settle in and feel comfortable in their environment before they start school.

There's nothing more stressful than when your child is disappointed and doesn't understand why things are different than planned. Moving can be hard enough and when our children anticipate a particular timeline, it's important to be the guide by their sides to do our best to meet their expectations. That way everyone is more comfortable with the transition.

Regulations and Requirements

Another situation is when people have investment property and want to do a 1031 exchange. There's a specific time limit to identify up to three properties to move the proceeds and any debt to avoid a huge tax liability. The proceeds from the sale of the original investment property must go directly to an accommodator; the entity that holds your money until you purchase a replacement property. When you're in a strong seller's market, you want to work with someone who has the foresight to think ahead, keeping in mind what you are wanting to accomplish.

If you should make the mistake taking possession of the proceeds from the original investment property sale at closing, you will have forfeited the 1031 exchange. You just gave up the right to transfer the proceeds to another property and you have created a tax consequence. Anything to do with the IRS always elevates stress!

The other situation under regulations that I've seen people not understand is when you're working with clients that are not US residents. The IRS tax withholding laws is known as FIRPTA. This law states that the seller is going to have up to 15% withheld of the purchase price regardless if they have that much equity or not. Imagine getting all the way to that last one hundred yards and realizing you're not going to sell because you can't even afford to sell. You'd have to bring cash to the table to sell or you're not getting the cash up front to go to that next place. Yet, if you work with real estate advisors, like us, that have helped people internationally, you know that there are documents helping you to plan ahead and then you'll know the exact amount that is owed.

These are the kind of stresses that working with a guide by your side are able to alleviate because we've helped sellers through many different complex situations. That way you're not experiencing those painful mistakes and just a bad, those costly mistakes.

The Unknown

When I am facing something unknown it's important to me that I know there is safety and security, that way I can feel comfortable. With all things that are unknown to us, things that we need take care of, get done that's where having a guide by our side is necessary. It is critical having a skilled professional who can react to what is and come up with creative solutions so that we continue moving forward. This is the opposite of going, "Oh no!!!", creating drama or wasting time complaining about what happened. A guide can actually step up and say "This is what happened, this is how we can resolve it…are you good with that?" or "here are two other choices, which would you prefer?" Meanwhile they are continuing in that forward progress.

DID YOU KNOW?

The Average Real Estate agent is involved in

ONLY one transaction a year?

Situations with Unique Variables and Specific Timelines Affecting Complexity

Probate

We've help those who find themselves responsible for real estate a loved one leaves behind and if you should find yourself in this situation, you can feel comfortable that we understand what everyone is dealing with as well as real estate and can be a real resource especially now. In the meantime, this is a story about a personal representative and his experience:

One day I got a call from Bill who lives in Virginia. He was in town because his brother, Robert, had passed away two weeks ago. Bill was the personal representative and only heir of his brother's estate. As the personal representative, he was in charge of handling all the details of the estate. Bill was referred to us by his attorney, Paul, who was handling the probate process. As you can imagine, it was a very emotional time for Bill who was dealing with the loss of his brother. He was grieving and also feeling overwhelmed because there were so many things to handle. He needed to get Robert's home prepared because he didn't want to have to carry the expense of the home and was hoping to sell quickly.

While there were many tactical details that needed to be addressed to prepare the home for sale, Bill really needed someone who was an expert, was patient and would listen intently to exactly what he needed throughout the process. Bill needed to work with a real estate advisor with strong communication skills, someone that he could trust, to reduce his stress of not being here while the home was for sale. We also helped Bill to "press the easy button" of selling by using our email electronic signature program for ease of signing all the documents long distance

Bill was only in town for a short amount of time. Because we do this every day, we guided him through what to expect to relieve the overwhelm with our step-by step-plan for getting this home prepared, marketed and successfully sold. We helped him gain clarity and prioritize what to do first using our room-by-room review process. We helped Bill focus on what he would take with him, what would stay in the house, what would be donated to charity, and what would be discarded.

He was able to leave shortly after choosing my team and me to help him; feeling confident that we had it handled, we had his back, and he could relax because everything would go smoothly. We utilized our unique listing marketing strategy and with the home prepared, staged, photographed and ready for the next family we received several offers and it quickly went under contract.

Bill was very relieved and appreciative of the way we could lead, guide and protect him through the process, making it as painless as possible and protecting the estate's equity.

1031 exchange

Our job as real estate advisors is to not only help prepare your home before going on the market, it's also to guide, lead and protect you so that your home sells for the highest price and best terms, as well as, on a timeline that works best for your move.

DID YOU KNOW?

When doing a 1031 Exchange You ONLY have 45 Days

to Identify up to 3 Properties to Purchase

There are many ways to successfully complete a 1031 exchange and it's a tax-planning tool that sellers should not attempt on their own. It's important to obtain the advice of a CPA or tax professional before selling an investment property.

When sellers are planning to sell one investment property and roll into another qualifying property timing is paramount, because when you sell your current property two important things must happen.

1. Never touch any of the proceeds from the sale. All

the proceeds must go to a qualified intermediary or accommodator to remain qualified for the 1031 tax benefit.

2. The other is to completely understand the strict timeframe allowed.

Timing issues are very critical and understanding all the implications of timing can save or cost you thousands of dollars. It's even more important when you're selling in a sellers' market with fewer investments to buy because when you sell your current investment property it's very likely it will sell quickly. Then the IRS gives you a mere 45 days to identify a maximum of three properties as options to purchase. If you cannot successfully close on one of the three identified properties then you have lost the benefit. If you miss the 45-day deadline to identify properties, you may have lost the benefit of deferring your taxes owed from this sale.

If you cannot successfully close on one of the three identified properties within six months of the sale of your original investment property, then again you have lost the benefits of the 1031 exchange option.

Plus, you will still need to pay the accommodator their fee, and you will be extremely disappointed.

the plan of finding those properties and sometimes it makes sense to even negotiate on them before completing the sale on your original investment property. During seller markets with limited homes available for purchase, finding an investment property that matches your personal goals and requirements can be very challenging. If there is nothing out there you like, the only option you will have is to consider less desirable properties or lose the tax benefit and pay the IRS money due on the gain.

We've helped many of our clients start looking early so that once their investment property sold, they were ready and able to make the right moves, in the right timeframes, and they did not have the stress of owing the IRS a lot of money. Our experience helps us know what to look for to help owners who are selling and doing a 1031 exchange for the first time.

It's a Wrap

It's not unusual to want the treasure!
It's the prize at the end of the rainbow ...
It's the big hooray at end of the race ...
It's the box office hit at the end of the red carpet ...

And the preparation...the practice, the sweating, the falling down, the bandaging up bruised knees and ankles, the ice packs, the late-night planning for a new angle, the glitch in technology that prevents or delays a step, the needed doctor visit that delays time and eats into costs...all this is not what we want.

We all can relate to this part because somewhere we've experienced setbacks. When our eye is on the prize we want to catapult over the setbacks straight to victory.

This time you can...

Reach out and "press the easy button" and call me at 727-710-8035. My experienced team and I will help you get from where you are to where you want to be with ease and grace.

CHAPTER FOUR

Additional Resources:
Ten Questions to Ask Before Choosing a Real Estate Agent

If you're thinking about selling a home, one of the first things you'll need is an experienced real estate agent. Chances are you may already know one from within your own social circle or have received referrals from neighbors, friends, and family members. For those of you starting from scratch, online tools are also available and can provide extensive background to help you find your perfect match.

No matter how you decide to search for your agent, you'll need to know what to ask them before you begin your journey together. You are going to be spending a lot of time with your agent so his or her style had better be compatible with yours.

Do you need someone easygoing or someone aggressive? I imagine you like working with someone similar to yourself. You may want to work with someone with an easygoing personality, a great sense of humor or perhaps someone who is assertive. What is most important because you will be working with them over the next few months, is that you feel comfortable with that person.

Here are ten questions that you could ask your potential real estate agent or broker before you hire them to help you with the preparation, marketing and sale of your home:

1. What percentage of your clients are sellers vs. buyers? (A balance is helpful because you know what buyers want and also know what to look for in buyer offers when representing a seller)

2. Will I be working with you directly or handed off to anyone else other than you? In other words, will you handle all aspects of my transaction or will you delegate some tasks to a sales associate or administrative assistant? (A knowledgeable assistant can be invaluable to an agent, but you, the seller, want to make sure you can connect with your agent regularly.)

3. Do you work full-time or part-time as a real estate agent? (Now that you all that a real estate advisor should be doing for you - can you see that getting done to the standard you want with someone that is part-time?)

4. How many homes have you closed in the past year?

5. How many other sellers are you representing now?

6. How many buyers? (Hint: You want to make sure the agent or team you hire isn't so busy that you're just a number and lost in the shuffle. In this case bigger isn't always better.)

7. Is your license in good standing? (Check an agent's certification yourself with your state's Department of Real Estate. Many states provide this information online. For example, in Florida residents may check at www.myfloridalicense.com/ and click on Verify a License.)

8. How many years of education and experience do you have? (Experience and continuing education typically make for better agents.)

9. Are you also a Broker and/or a Realtor® or simply an agent?

10. Can you provide me with the names and phone numbers of past clients who have agreed to be references? (Insights from past customers can help you learn more about an agent and give you a greater comfort level.) We can gladly provide that and also have over 100 videos where past clients have shared their experience in a playlist on our YouTube Channel at www.youtube.com/user/cyndeehaydon

If the agents check off this list then you're on the right track. Use this list to compare agents. But one word of caution is this: Do not pick someone so close to you that you can't have a serious "straight talk" business conversation.

You need someone with whom you are comfortable asking any question and sharing all your concerns. And keep in mind that this person will at some point become quite intimate with your entire financial picture. Choose the most qualified person for the job that you think you'll work well with. The ideal person for you is:

- an experienced professional
- who knows your market
- acts in an ethical manner
- answers all of your questions
- addresses your concerns and
- most important, will listen to you and be your teammate throughout the entire process.

Photo Shoot Prep Checklist

Exterior: Front/Back

- Remove cars from driveway
- Close all windows
- Clean all windows
- Sweep walkways
- Pick up leaves/sticks/branches
- Put toys, bicycles away
- Store away seasonal décor
- Stow garden tools, supplies
- Remove all hoses
- Straighten and arrange deck furniture
- Clean pool area
- Stage for lifestyle with wine glasses, plants, pillows
- Freshen mulch if needed

Interior: Dining Room

- Straighten/push in dining chairs
- Add centerpiece
- Set the table for dinner when possible
- Add a vase of flowers
- Add a bottle of wine, glasses

Interior: Main Areas

- Remove personal items/photos
- Remove all visible clutter
- Open shades and blinds - clean windows
- Replace burned out light bulbs

- Tidy up or put away all children's toys
- Empty waste baskets
- Hide pet dishes/toys/beds
- Vacuum carpets
- Sweep hard floors
- Remove newspapers, mail
- Display attractive books
- Turn off televisions
- Turn on all lights
- Remove rugs
- Turn off all ceiling fans

Interior: Bedrooms

- Make the beds
- Arrange decorative pillows
- Put away clothing, shoes
- Clean under the bed
- Clear surfaces of clutter
- Remove floor rugs
- Neutral solid bedspread with accent pillows
- Something green – artificial potted flower or plant
- Open all windows and let light in

Interior: Kitchen

- Remove all items from refrigerator door
- Store food in cabinets
- De-clutter counters, stove, book shelves
- Stow small appliances
- Hide soaps, cleaning items
- Hide dish towels, sponges
- Clear sink of dishes

- Put away draining rack
- Organize items on open shelves
- Place bowl of fruit on counter
- Remove sink mats / rugs
- Turn on microwave light onto oven
- Turn on all under mount lighting
- Wipe down all appliances

Interior: Bathrooms

- Make the bathrooms sparkle
- Remove all bath rugs
- Hang fresh towels
- Clear counters of toiletries
- Clean mirrors
- Clean toilet and close lid
- Remove all items from tub & shower
- Remove trash cans and plungers
- Remove toilet paper roll
- Remove all soaps toothbrush personal items from counter and put under counter or out of site
- Fresh new white shower curtain often a plus

As a Real Estate Advisor, What Do I Do All Day?

It certainly is not as easy as it looks on TV. As a real estate advisor, my job is to manage all the people involved in a transaction, making sure that they do their job. I must quickly adapt to what needs to be done to keep the transaction moving forward and also respond in a timely manner to client needs.

So where to start? Explaining how I spend my time is like attempting to explain what a doctor or lawyer does all day. There's a lot more that goes into "treating patients" or "handling legal matters" and the same goes for my life of helping people prepare, market and successfully sell property.

From a consumer's first thought about making a real estate move to actually taking the leap (whether that means right now, next month or a year from now), as your advisor, I am incubator, initiator, action-taker, coordinator, scheduler, personal concierge, resource person, problem-solver, mediator, miracle worker (sort-of), red-tape cutter, advocate, transaction manager and chief make-it-happen officer.

These are the general categories:

- Advising
- Responding
- Scheduling showings and consultations

- Making contact
- Setting and attending appointments
- Negotiating offers and managing the sale
- Problem-solving
- Marketing

Because I gratefully have a team, I may delegate some of these roles, but as your transaction coordinator of all the details, nothing gets completed without my oversight and input into what needs to be done and how to get it done.

Of course, I have a workday, just like you, and because I have a well thought out systems-based business and for each client I draft a specific, strategic plan, most of my work is completed during normal business hours.

Responding

Theoretically, except for holidays, there are no official days off in real estate. I might have periods of times without any scheduled appointments, but there are always inquiries, emails and texts requiring a response. In our instant-response society, there really is little waiting until tomorrow. But, my clients come to trust me; my clients know that my team and I are working diligently towards their goals. Since part of our system includes a call or email every Tuesday, experience shows my clients rarely need to call or email me because they already know what is occurring.

When someone calls my office about a property, we respond. If other agents contact my office to ask questions about my clients listing or want to show one of our properties, we quickly get back to them. When an offer to purchase is received, and after I have reviewed and verified the information pertaining to the offer, I then contact my client to present it.

The workplace is anywhere I am and although I have my team in the office during normal business hours, on-call virtually on Saturday, it means I don't have to be in the office for the day to start — work happens at home, in the car, during vacations and on the go.

The job often begins early in the morning when I begin follow-up email communications, phone calls and texts about any number of things. You would find me sitting with my laptop and cell phone obtaining showing feedback on listings, following-up on in-progress transactions, updating clients on recent activity, answering questions and addressing any concerns, and creating to-do lists for myself and my assistants.

Scheduling Showings and Consultations

One of my team members will put together property itineraries for our homebuyer clients who are planning a house hunting trip. This usually involves numerous showings in a short period of time.

Scheduling these tours requires a delicate dance that takes into consideration geography and logistics against the backdrop of unknown time constraints that sellers may impose. ("Can you come at 2 p.m. instead of 10 a.m.?" or "Today's not good, but how about Friday?")

These impromptu changes in plan wouldn't be a problem if my partner and I didn't have anything else to do. Some of our buyers have the luxury of time and they were local — but I'm rarely working with that kind of flexibility. And Murphy's Law says the property that's causing the scheduling difficulties will be the one at the top of our buyers' wish list. We always find a way to make it happen. But, while I'm sharing this, you as the home seller can consider how important it is to your success to be super flexible and willing to allow showings even at inconvenient times.

Setting and Attending Appointments

Then there are the appointments — meeting buyers and sellers for initial consultations, previewing and touring properties, meeting inspectors, meeting appraisers and a plethora of specialists, contractors, stagers, photographers and repair professionals.

While out on these meetings, business carries on and the emails, calls and texts flood in. Oftentimes my team and I will be juggling these meetings with the sellers from six months ago who call and want to meet immediately — or the buyer couple who suddenly found the perfect home that they need to see right away.

Negotiating Offers and Managing the Sale

The ever-important skill of negotiating offers may go on for days. Once an offer gets worked out and a property goes under contract, that is just the beginning of the next step. There's no jumping up and down, high-fiving and laughing all the way to the bank. Quite the contrary, this is where the next step of managing all the transactional details begins.

At this point, we have to make sure that everyone involved in this process does their job. From whatever side of the transaction they represent — buyer or seller — we need to make sure everyone is fulfilling their obligations of the transaction in a timely manner.

When a lender is involved, active and frequent communication is a must to ensure the loan process remains on track. We check in with the title company to verify the file is being handled and all details are being attended to. The team also address's anything unexpected that may arise and things always arise. But having an experienced real estate advisor, like me, will prove invaluable and make things as simple as possible…for you.

There are an endless number of tasks that must get done from contract to close, from reminding clients about utility transfers to ensuring the seller has everything moved out on the day so that we can hand over the keys to the buyer.

Problem-Solving

Problem-solving and crisis management happens at every turn. It includes educating my clients about the realities of what they are trying to accomplish, running down information about a community, association or property, and troubleshooting umpteen potential issues that could derail the transaction and ultimately the closing.

Unlike many jobs, one of the things that I love most is that no two days are the same. One week could be plagued by multiple snags (a buyer's financing falls apart, home inspection issues, etc.), and on another day, it all comes together in an eerily smooth manner. There is no guarantee that the time spent and the hours that my team and I put in will result in a paycheck.

I can't bill for the time and effort expended giving advice, giving accurate information, showing properties, attending inspections and appraisals, preparing for open house events and more. I work on a contingent basis and will only be reimbursed monetarily for all the team efforts when the home is sold. The other way I am compensated is when my outrageously happy client introduces me to their friends, family members, coworkers, you know, the people that they care about, who could use my help.

Marketing

Another part of the process is the marketing and business development. I pour my heart into my brand, my knowledge and my expertise. I have websites, newsletters, postcards, videos or other marketing pieces drawing attention to my sellers' homes and our ability to prepare, and sell homes. I devote thought and resources to each marketing piece with an eye toward implementation, execution and tracking results at every turn.

In short, real estate is a profession full of follow-up, follow-up, follow-up; multi-tasking, prioritizing, re-prioritizing; evaluating, advising and coaching, guiding, researching and problem-solving, and the ever-important communication.

Despite what reality television portrays, I don't simply ride around in an expensive car. I won't show up in designer clothes at some swanky place to negotiate a deal over trendy cocktails. It might appear glamorous and easy, yet showing some properties or putting a home on the market happens sometime in the middle of a very involved process. Marketing, branding and creating top-of-mind presence usually comes first, and those are the things along with the proven results and introduction from happy clients that motivate customers to choose my team.

Real estate advisors, like me, are the catalyst for the entire process of preparing, marketing and successfully selling. And guiding clients from where they are to where they want to be is always at the forefront of what I do.

Additional Before and After Photos:

I was able to share several examples of Before and After photos earlier in the book and wanted to add a few more here to give you more inspiration and awareness. Maybe you'll even get a stronger visual sense of what I mean when I say, "that how you live in a home is not how you sell a house."

Here are examples of preparation and staging transformations we've done for clients we've helped. You can see the dramatic impact of our detailed preparation process and how we set the stage and are able to get real buyers to offer our clients the most money for one of your biggest assets.

Bathroom Before

Bathroom After

Teenager's Bedroom Before

Teenager's Bedroom After

Vacant Master Bedroom Before

Vacant Master Bedroom After

Florida Room Before

Florida Room with Carpet Removed - Stage 2

Florida Room Decluttered - After

Florida Room After Soft Staging

Living Room Before

Living Room After

Living Room Before

Living Room After

Entryway Before

Entryway After

Formal Living Room Before

Formal Living Room After

Kitchen Before

Kitchen After

Kitchen Before

Kitchen After

Florida Room Before

Florida Room After

Florida Room Before

Florida Room After

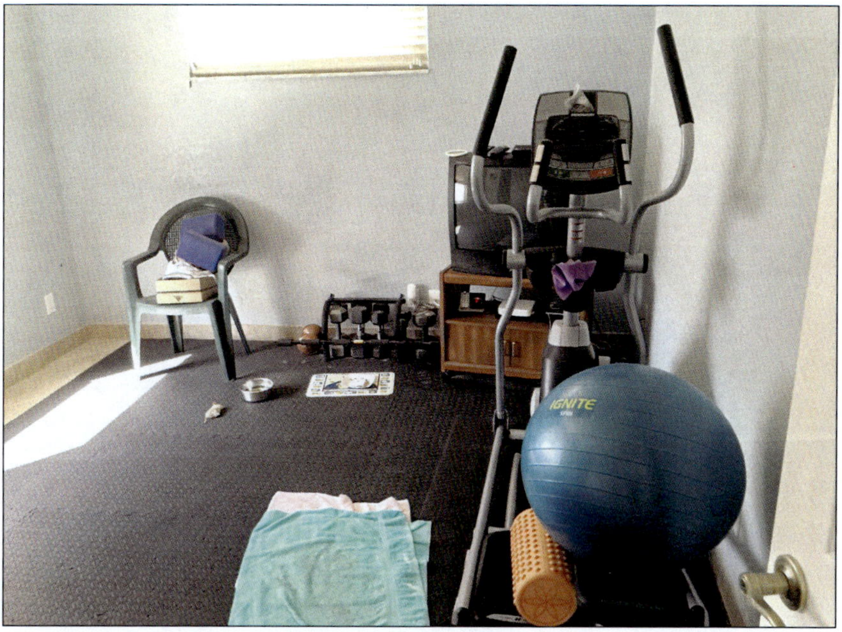

Home Gym Before

Home Gym After

Patio Before

Patio After

Bonus Area in Master Bedroom Room Before

Bonus Area in Master Bedroom Room After

Living Room Before

Living Room After

Showcasing Lifestyle

Showcasing Lifestyle

Showcasing Lifestyle

Showcasing Lifestyle

Showcasing Lifestyle

Showcasing Lifestyle

Raving Fans: Helping People on The Move

This has been such a process and Cyndee basically she held our hands all the way through. We're so thankful for her and being able to negotiate with the with the sellers. We had a lot of interesting and difficult issues like we had issue with the tree and whether it was possible to be able to build a pool or not and she helped us with the zoning items and with everything. She just become our friend and we built this really trusting relationship with her and are very, very thankful for Cyndee. I had the opportunity to deal with all kinds of different Realtors as a former banker and Cyndee was above and beyond all of my expectations that I dealt with in the past, thank you!

Charlie and I are so fortunate that we met up with Cyndee Haydon and it's been over six years now since she first helped us with the purchase of our Beach condo and worked with us for two solid years until we found the perfect place. She did such a great job that we had enough confidence to have our house listed with her. This was our home that we've been in for over 22 years, so it was a very big decision but Cyndee did such a great job.

She's detail-oriented and she knows her stuff and that was so important to us because. She knows the law she knows about all the potential issues so when we decided to put the house up for sale a good year in advance Cyndee got a great inspector to come in and look at the house and check everything out that we needed to update or have repaired so we did that and we worked on that got all the necessary things done then we listed the house with Cyndee. At that point, she came in and she went room by room and helped us figure out what we needed to get rid of and how we needed to stage the home and that was quite a long process.

Thank You Cyndee for doing that because it made all the difference. She then brought in professional photographer who did a fantastic job he took still pictures he did the video walkthrough he even brought a drone and to go up and down the canal these just made all the difference in the marketing that Cyndee was able to do. The house and photos showed beautifully and that helped immensely with the sale.

Cyndee did a super job on all communication involved and if any question that may come up at any particular time in the transaction it was wonderful to be able to have that expertise available all the time and she did a fantastic job.

– Ellen and Charlie Whitaker

As a young first-time home-seller, I truly had no idea what to expect while forging into the unknown territory that often accompanies the daunting process. As any hesitant person would, I took to the internet searching through pages and pages of tips, guidelines, and recommendations for those trained specifically in the art of reality. Living in Clearwater, FL, I noticed how saturated the webpages were with Realtors and reviews, often leading to mixed experiences that didn't leave me confident with entrusting such a significant task to any one person. Then, the reviews for Cyndee and Jack Haydon graced my screen.

After reading positive review after positive review, my husband and I decided to call Cyndee to conduct a phone interview in order to see if she was a suitable candidate. Rather than provide us with a generic overview, she went out of her way to come to our location immediately, tour our house and walk us through her unique process. From the start, it was obvious that her loyalty to clients naturally expelled, and that she was extremely passionate about her career. Cyndee answered all questions we had, and proved exceptionally knowledgeable about the process from beginning to end.

Once we agreed to follow her advice, she went about teaching us how to properly stage our home, advertise and ultimately hook our buyer. She hired a phenomenal professional photographer to capture the unique beauty and character of our house, and created a webpage to showcase our property. She used her skills and discernment to build a mountain of interest in our property, before allowing an Open House, bringing in over 50 potential buyers in a single afternoon. That Open House was the only one needed; because of Cyndee's talent we accepted a superb offer and were under contact in less than 24 hours!

Her hard work didn't stop then, as she was on top of all communication, documents, and legal measures leading up to the signing table. Cyndee was never farther than a phone call away, and proved to us that her business and reputation are truly something to be respected and admired. It is with the upmost confidence that I recommend Cyndee Haydon for absolutely any realty need.

– **Alexia and Alex Ronay**

As a probate attorney, I represent family members who are left to deal with assets and debts of a deceased relative. When death comes unexpectedly, those family members have the unenviable responsibility of making legal and business decisions while in a state of shock and grief. Along with providing legal advice, it is important that I represent my clients with compassion and empathy during this very difficult time.

A person's residence is often the most valuable asset one owns. After death, the payment of the debts and administration costs may require the surviving family to sell the residence. My experience has been that the best way to maximize the value and sales price of a residence is to work with a professional real estate broker as part of the probate team. When I make a recommendation to my clients to use a broker, I know that any referrals will reflect on me, and I must be very careful to refer only those individuals who share my same level of professionalism.

Cyndee Haydon is an excellent example of a real estate professional who I am always confident and happy to refer to my clients. I know that when Cyndee is involved my clients are in excellent hands, I know the job will get done and I know the value of the residence will be maximized.

Cyndee recently was asked to help with an estate of a gentleman who passed away unexpectedly. His brother was in charge of administering the probate administration. The house needed to be sold, but the brother had work obligations and was not able to give much attention to preparing the house for sale. Cyndee came in and understood my client's predicament and took control of the entire process of the sale. She started by uncluttering the house to be more presentable. Cyndee arranged for staging professional photos. This was followed up with an entire marketing campaign specifically for this house. Shortly thereafter, the estate received an excellent purchase offer. During the entire process, Cyndee maintained regular communications with the client, the title company and our office. Everyone was always on the same page throughout. The client was thrilled and relieved to have had someone to lean on during this difficult time.

Cyndee is committed to providing her clients, as well as everyone else involved, an excellent experience. This is especially true when she is representing probate clients. Cyndee is compassionate and empathetic in the difficult time of probate administration. Her overall professionalism and deep personal connection with her clients is what sets her apart from other real estate professionals.

– Peter Rivellini

The first thing that I think is quite unique about Cyndee as a real estate broker is she works hard and not only has all the local knowledge but also countrywide. She works at building and maintaining relationships with not only her clients but with people that may offer skill and expertise to her clients when they have specific needs or problems that arises in any real estate transaction.

To offer an example, she has many contacts in the construction industry, lawyers and Chamber of Commerce people. She's always going to seminars and attending meetings where things are brought up about the future in real estate in by tapping into that and knowing the market she obviously has the skills to do a valuation of anybody's home and here they are in the market and what is the best price is.

Developing these relationships is something that I've not seen other brokers do as well as Cyndee and when she needs something and she has a list of go to people and they are the cream of the crop for a homeowner that is trying to sell a property and they are responsive too.

The second thing is when you have the house to sell, she is excellent at preparing you and preparing your property so that it will show well and get the best price. She not only advises her clients as to how to set up the house and get rid of clutter which we all have but she gets right in there and helps do it. I was in New Hampshire and when I was selling my property here in Florida and she did it all, set up everything that needed to be done, she brings in her own accoutrements if she needs to, little touches that helped create an environment that sells the house and that's why she sold my house in like 11 days which was quite a surprise to me and then I realized I didn't have a home to come home to.

But that's one of the things when she does videos and still photos and brochures is she has a wonderful eye for color, for style and for presentation and that's really important when you're selling your property. You have no idea until you see the difference between what my house looked like before Cyndee came and what it looked like after she staged it.

And the third thing is her communication skills and she leaves absolutely nothing to chance. She communicates with you constantly. In fact, you've seen the gunslinger in old Westerns that had a pistol in each hand, well Cyndee has a telephone in each hand and she carries them with her so that she is always available to her clients or anyone else that she is asking for assistance from or needs her help. She's always available and answers you right away when you have a need and is very reassuring.

The other thing about her communication skills is when she calls you because some glitch has come up and the transaction, she doesn't just give you the bad news. She always gives you some solution, some alternatives so that you can think about how you want to handle it, what you need to do and never just leaves you with the bad news so that not you're worried about making your sale.

I think these are important attributes and I was a former broker myself in the 1970's and while lots of things certainly have changed I think that's what makes her excel in her business. She also becomes your friend and part of your family which is really important if you have a real estate transaction which is why I recommend her.

– **Dawn Barrett**

We have been investing in real estate for a couple of years now. We are actively adding to our portfolio of rentals, as well as flipping houses when we find the right opportunities. It's too bad we didn't engage with Cyndee before our last flip!

After having successfully completed one profitable flip, we bought a house that needed total rehab. The Realtor we were working with encouraged us to improve the house a lot more than the market would bear. As an investor & seller we of course wanted to sell the house and make as much as possible. We were really depending on the Realtor expertise of the market & marketing skills. After a year on the market, with a lot of showing but, no real reasons of why the buyers were not buying. We were losing money monthly for insurance, staging, landscaping, etc., we knew we needed a change. Although we liked our Realtor personally, we hadn't gotten any meaningful offers during that whole year! We were not happy investors! We decided to give a more experienced Realtor a call.

Cyndee had helped us find just the right home for us when we first moved to the St. Pete area a few years ago. We gave her a call to see if she could give us some advice on how we should proceed in selling the Rehabbed property. Cyndee came loaded with tons of information on the area, how the market was improving & how to proceed with overcoming objections from buyers. After Cyndee listed & showed the house several times we had a much better idea what buyers were looking for & the objections they had. She secured a contract within the 1st two months. Unfortunately, that contract fell thru, ostensibly due to an item not passing inspection. The reality was that the buyers simply got cold feet. We had two more offers and Cyndee secured a backup offer that was actually better for us (thanks to her strong negotiating skills), and we closed on the house shortly after. Thank you, Cyndee!

Here are some things that Cyndee helped us with that made all the difference:

- ☐ She didn't pull punches, giving us her honest opinion on who the right buyer would be and how to properly position the property.
- ☐ Cyndee's marketing machine made sure that buyers understood the value of the separate-entranced in-law suite, appealing to an artist, someone wanting a detached office, a first-time buyer being able to use

the potential rental income from the separate unit to help with down payment assistance.

- Emphasized the advantages of location like: desirable location; no flood insurance; good schools.
- Strong marketing knowledge, professional photos and proper marketing and positioning.
- She helped us get tradespeople and inspectors when issues arose to keep the transaction moving forward, while still being sensitive to the fact that this was an investment property.

Throughout the process, Cyndee always kept us informed. Whenever there were issues, she brought advice and solutions based on her experience to reach a successful conclusion. This was especially appreciated when we left the country for an extended trip in Europe. She and Jack took care of everything while we were traveling, including managing all the transaction details.

Our latest adventure? Cyndee just helped us put a contract on another house that we plan to do some minor rehab on and hold it as another rental.

As you consider stepping into the world of real estate investment, make sure you have a strong resource you can lean on!

Linda & Rick Sandler
Makeitso Investment Group

We had already moved into our new house before we started the process of selling our then empty house. I contacted Cyndee and she was very helpful and walked me through the process as a first-time seller and we got the house on the market within a week.

Cyndee went above and beyond to make sure that the house looked great for showing to potential buyers by staging the house with props and furniture. As a Realtor, she was able to obtain feedback from potential buyers looking at the property which helped us identify areas of weakness that we adjusted before the next showings.

She also came with a team of people we could use to get the house in tip-top shape – cleaning crew, landscaping, and pressure washer- to make sure that my house sparkled. All of Cyndee's efforts went beyond that of a basic listing agent; her staging work and social media campaign made such a positive impact on buyers that the house sold within a month for nearly the entire asking price. – **Laura Snell Johnson**

My wife Emily and I bought a house here in Clearwater Beach in 2010. Cyndee and Jack were our Realtors during that process and helped us buy the house and it was great. We had a great five and a half years here in the house and we live remotely so we use the house for our own vacation use and as a rental income and loved every minute of it but life has changed.

We haven't been able to use it much in the last few years and so we decided to put the house on the market and Cyndee and Jack were there for us to help us every step of the way.

They put together a really nice comprehensive plan. They had great market knowledge here in a Clearwater Beach area for us and really showed us the comparables and gave us a lot of really good tips on how to make the house the most attractive for a new buyer and then really helped us in the details because again we don't live here in the area.

They did a lot of the legwork for us to get the house ready put a comprehensive plan together for us and we were very happy that we stuck to the plan and we've sold our house. We're very happy and it's been a really painless process. I couldn't ask for more from a real estate team than Jack and Cyndee and really happy that we used them both on the purchase and on the sale.

- **Steve and Emily Walton**

Cyndee and Jack was referred to us by our agent in Knoxville TN, they are just very nice and awesome agents, they will work on your schedule, she will do everything to make your house sellable.

Believe me, we just sold our last month, we had an open house on the 8th of October and we sold our house in 5 days, very amazing. We thank God that he gave us very hard-working agents. Very thankful to Cyndee and Jack. If anyone looking for a hard-working agent that you can trust, Cyndee and Jack Haydon are the right agents

– **Michel-Rene and Merlita Lloyd**

Having dealt with quite a few realtors over the years, I don't take recommendations lightly when it comes to recommending realtors to my family and friends. Cyndee and Jack Haydon are phenomenal realtors who both helped us buy our dream home near the beach in Pinellas County and helped us sell a home in New Tampa.

Both transactions had many complexities and Cyndee and Jack navigated us through to a successful close like the experts they truly are. From negotiating the contract, to dealing with the complexities of a VA loan, including the VA appraisal process, effectively and continuously communi.cating with the seller's lender, and overall ensuring that we received more money in our pocket than we would have with ANY OTHER REALTOR,

I wholeheartedly believe that their expertise compares to none in the field. Cyndee and Jack represented us like no other realtors we have found to date, and will be our realtors for all of our future real estate deals. So many realtors do not treat their job as a full-time job and simply expect their commission to fall into their pocket.

Not only do Cyndee and Jack WORK HARD, but they are committed to continuing education and expertise in their field, allowing them to close the most complex transactions.

– **Meghan and Stephen Theodore**

Having Cyndee Haydon as our Realtor for the sale of our Clearwater Beach home was a pure pleasure! She handled each step in our home sale with integrity, professionalism and with great results.

From the staging and marketing of our home to the open houses and showings through the negotiations, inspections and closing, Cyndee was consistently on top of any issue or problem that arose. With her substantial knowledge, extensive background and in-depth experience in real estate, she seamlessly guided us through each area of our real estate transaction.

And throughout our dealings, she was always upbeat, enthusiastic, encouraging and extremely helpful. Effective and timely communications is Cyndee's hallmark. Without any reservation, we most highly recommend Cyndee Haydon to anyone seeking to buy or sell a home. She is truly outstanding and unparalleled in the real estate field! Don't look anywhere else!

– **Joanne and Dick Schickel**

I found Jack and Cyndee Haydon online on Yelp doing my research and it was a great experience. They not only sold my home quickly, they also helped me with getting the home ready to be sold and actually even helped me find people to get all the things done so we could get it on the market as quickly as possible.

We had relocated to Georgia already and it was so helpful to have them there to handle everything. I was up there and not having to worry about what was happening down here. When we got everything done and it sold very fast. A lot of people don't realize what an important piece this is of getting top dollar and people will nickel and dime you if not.

My advice to other sellers is to be patient and be flexible and know it will get done smoothly with Jack and Cyndee.

\- **Mike Vitale**

We enjoyed working with Cyndee Haydon. She helped us sell our home in Clearwater Florida and purchase a new home in Oldsmar and she was excellent to work with helping us prepare our home for a buyer she worked diligently to market our home and showed our home frequently and was very encouraging to us and helping us stage our home we really appreciate all that Cyndee and her team have done for us,

- Amy and Brad Stewart

ABOUT THE AUTHOR

Cyndee Haydon moved every 2 years growing up including her Senior year and attended the University of Florida and majored in Computer Science Business where she started working for IBM, which is only fitting with her history of "I've Been Moved".

After college Cyndee continued working for IBM where she met her husband, Jack in 1985. Their last IBM move brought them to Tampa and when IBM said their next job was in Dallas, they decided "NO" because people work their whole lives to live here in paradise and that is how their real estate business was born.

Since 2005, Cyndee and her husband, Jack, as partners have helped hundreds of families happily and successfully buy and sell properties. Cyndee is a caring, committed, real estate advisor who has earned the following designations and certifications to better help their clients: Certified Professional Property Stager, Certified Luxury Home

Marketing Specialist, Pricing Strategy Advisor, Certified International Property Specialist, Resort and Second Home Property Specialist, Military Relocation Specialist and Seller Representative Specialist. A proven leader in the Tampa Bay real estate community, consistently ranking in the Top 5% or above of all local Realtors®. Cyndee Serves on both her local and state Board of Directors and is known for being a strong champion for homeowners, especially in the area of Flood Insurance.

Cyndee's life philosophy influences everything she does. It's the "can do" approach to any challenge, coupled with her positive attitude, that contributes to building a successful real estate business.

Cyndee says, "When you really love what you do, it doesn't feel like work. The trust that comes from working with our clients makes the help my team and I provide the most rewarding part of my job."

Maybe that's why 95% of the people they help today are repeat clients and new clients introduced by those that have been help by her and her team in the past.

Cyndee Haydon's Memberships and Designations

- SRS - Seller Representative Specialist
- CPPS - Certified Professional Property Stager Realtor Consultant
- PSA - Pricing Strategy Advisor
- CLHMS - Certified Luxury Home Marketing Specialist
- CIPS - Certified International Property Specialist
- RSPS - Resort and Second Property Specialist
- MRP - Military Relocation Professional

- SRF - Short Sale and Foreclosure Resource
- Member of Pinellas Realtor Organization, the Florida Realtors Organization and National Association of REALTORS®
- Member of By Referral Only and BroVance

Advocating for clients, neighbors and communities:

- Awarded First District 6 Leadership Institute Hall of Fame Award 2017
- Awarded Florida Realtors Honor Society
- Recipient of Pinellas Realtor Organization Service Award
- Florida Realtors® Leadership Academy Graduate
- Florida Realtors® Board of Directors
- Florida Realtors® Public Policy Committee & Chair of Insurance Subcommittee
- President Elect, Leadership Pinellas
- Pinellas Realtor Board of Directors
- Pinellas Realtor Organization Public Policy Chair
- Pinellas Realtor RPAC Chair
- Pinellas County Sheriff's Citizen's Academy Graduate

Reach Cyndee at:

- *727-710-8035*
- *Cyndee@SandbarsToSunsets.com*

Made in United States
North Haven, CT
05 November 2026

21763975R60077